The Khmer Empire

An In-Depth Exploration of Southeast Asia's Great Civilization

By

Suraj Matthai

Table of Content

Introduction

Welcome to the Khmer Empire

Brief Introduction to the Khmer Empire and Its Significance

Welcome to the fascinating world of the Khmer Empire, one of Southeast Asia's greatest civilizations. Flourishing between the 9th and 15th centuries, the Khmer Empire was a powerful and influential kingdom centered in present-day Cambodia. Renowned for its architectural masterpieces, the Khmer Empire's capital, Angkor, became the site of some of the most iconic temples and structures in the world, including the majestic Angkor Wat and the enigmatic Bayon Temple.

The Khmer Empire's significance extends beyond its monumental architecture. It was a beacon of cultural, religious, and technological advancements. The empire's sophisticated irrigation systems and agricultural techniques supported a thriving economy and a large population. Moreover, the Khmer's artistic achievements, particularly in sculpture and bas-relief, remain awe-inspiring and provide a window into the spiritual and cultural life of the period.

Purpose and Scope of the eBook

This eBook aims to offer an in-depth exploration of the Khmer Empire, delving into its rich history, society, culture, and lasting legacy. By tracing the rise and fall of this remarkable civilization, we seek to provide readers with a comprehensive understanding of what made the Khmer Empire a pivotal force in Southeast Asian history.

The scope of this eBook encompasses the key aspects that defined the Khmer Empire:

- Its historical evolution from a small kingdom to a dominant empire.
- The intricate political and social structures that governed daily life.
- The profound religious transformations and practices that shaped Khmer spirituality.
- The architectural and artistic achievements that continue to captivate the world.
- The economic systems and trade networks that fueled its prosperity.
- The factors that led to its decline and the enduring legacy it left behind.

Overview of What Readers Will Learn

In this eBook, readers will embark on a journey through the various facets of the Khmer Empire. Each chapter is designed to provide detailed insights into specific aspects of this grand civilization:

1. **The Rise of the Khmer Empire** - Discover the origins, early history, and key figures who propelled the Khmer Empire to greatness.
2. **Society and Culture** - Explore the social hierarchy, daily life, religious practices, and the Khmer language and literature.
3. **Architectural Marvels** - Gain a deeper appreciation for the iconic temples of Angkor Wat, Angkor Thom, and other significant structures.
4. **Art and Iconography** - Delve into the artistic styles, sculptures, and bas-reliefs that tell the stories of deities and mythological events.
5. **Economy and Trade** - Understand the agricultural practices, trade routes, and economic activities that sustained the empire.
6. **The Fall of the Khmer Empire** - Analyze the internal and external factors that led to the empire's decline and its impact on subsequent history.

By the end of this eBook, readers will have a holistic view of the Khmer Empire, appreciating its contributions to world heritage and recognizing the importance of preserving its legacy. Whether you are a history enthusiast, a student, or simply curious about one of the world's most intriguing ancient civilizations, this eBook promises to enrich your knowledge and inspire further exploration.

Part 1

The Rise of the Khmer Empire

Chapter 1

Historical Context

Origins of the Khmer People

The origins of the Khmer people trace back to ancient migrations and settlements in Southeast Asia. The Khmer, an ethnic group native to Cambodia, have a history that predates the rise of the Khmer Empire by several centuries. Archaeological evidence suggests that the region was inhabited as early as the Neolithic period, with early Khmer societies engaging in farming, fishing, and rudimentary forms of trade. These early communities laid the foundation for the complex and sophisticated civilization that would later emerge.

The Khmer people are believed to have originated from the Mon-Khmer language family, which is part of the larger Austroasiatic linguistic group. This connection places them in a broader context of regional migrations and interactions with neighboring cultures.˙ As the Khmer people settled in the fertile plains surrounding the Tonle Sap Lake and the Mekong River, they developed agricultural practices that would sustain their growing population and set the stage for future developments.

Early History and the Formation of the Khmer Empire

The early history of the Khmer people is marked by the establishment of small, independent polities that gradually coalesced into more centralized forms of governance. By the 1st century CE, the region saw the rise of the Kingdom of Funan, an influential early civilization that played a crucial role in the region's development. Funan's strategic location along maritime trade routes allowed it to interact with Indian, Chinese, and other Southeast Asian cultures, leading to significant cultural and technological exchanges.

The decline of Funan in the 6th century gave rise to the Kingdom of Chenla, which further consolidated power in the region. Chenla's influence extended over much of present-day Cambodia, Laos, and southern Vietnam. This period saw the development of early Khmer art, architecture, and religious practices, which were heavily influenced by Indian culture, particularly Hinduism and Buddhism.

The true formation of the Khmer Empire began in the early 9th century under the leadership of Jayavarman II, often considered the founding father of the empire. In 802 CE, Jayavarman II declared himself the "universal monarch" (chakravartin) and established the capital at Hariharalaya near the present-day city of Siem Reap. This event marked the beginning of the Angkorian period and the unification of various Khmer polities into a cohesive empire.

Key Figures in the Rise of the Empire

Several key figures played pivotal roles in the rise of the Khmer Empire, shaping its development and expansion:

- **Jayavarman II**: As the founder of the Khmer Empire, Jayavarman II's reign was crucial in establishing the political and religious foundations of the empire. His declaration of divine kingship and unification of disparate regions set the stage for future prosperity.
- **Indravarman I**: Succeeding Jayavarman II, Indravarman I continued to expand the empire's territory and influence. He initiated significant construction projects, including the Preah Ko temple and the Bakong temple, the latter being one of the earliest examples of temple-mountain architecture.
- **Yasovarman I**: Known for founding the city of Yasodharapura, which would later become Angkor, Yasovarman I's reign saw the expansion of the empire's infrastructure. He constructed the Eastern Baray, a massive reservoir that exemplified the Khmer's advanced engineering skills in water management.
- **Suryavarman II**: Perhaps the most famous Khmer king, Suryavarman II is credited with constructing the magnificent Angkor Wat, a temple complex that remains one of the world's most significant architectural achievements. His reign marked the zenith of the Khmer Empire's power and cultural influence.

- **Jayavarman VII**: A pivotal figure in the later period of the empire, Jayavarman VII is known for his military prowess and extensive building projects, including the Bayon temple and Ta Prohm. He was also a devout Buddhist, which led to the increased prominence of Buddhism in the empire.

These leaders, through their vision and ambition, transformed the Khmer Empire into a formidable force in Southeast Asia. Their contributions to the empire's political stability, architectural grandeur, and cultural richness continue to be celebrated and studied to this day.

Chapter 2

Political Structure

Governance and Administration

The governance and administration of the Khmer Empire were highly centralized, with a well-defined hierarchy that facilitated effective control over its vast territories. The empire was divided into several provinces, each overseen by a local governor appointed by the king. These governors were responsible for maintaining order, collecting taxes, and ensuring the king's edicts were followed. The administrative system was supported by a network of officials, scribes, and local leaders who managed day-to-day affairs and reported directly to the central authority.

The Khmer administration also employed a sophisticated system of record-keeping and bureaucracy. The use of inscriptions on temple walls and other monuments provided detailed accounts of royal decrees, religious activities, and important events. This meticulous record-keeping helped maintain the coherence of the empire and facilitated communication across its extensive territories.

Role of the King and the Royal Court

At the heart of the Khmer Empire's political structure was the king, who wielded absolute power and was considered a divine ruler. The king's authority was legitimized through religious rituals and the concept of divine kingship, where the monarch was seen as a god-king, an earthly representative of the divine. This belief was reinforced by grandiose temple constructions and religious ceremonies that emphasized the king's sacred status.

The royal court, composed of nobles, priests, and advisors, played a crucial role in supporting the king's rule. The court was a center of political activity, where decisions regarding governance, military campaigns, and religious matters were made. High-ranking officials and members of the nobility were often given significant administrative responsibilities and lands in exchange for their loyalty and service to the king.

Priests and religious leaders held considerable influence in the royal court, guiding the king on spiritual and moral matters. The intertwining of religion and politics was a defining feature of the Khmer Empire, with the king often acting as both a temporal and spiritual leader. This dual role reinforced the king's authority and helped maintain social order and cohesion within the empire.

Military Organization and Expansion

The military organization of the Khmer Empire was a key factor in its ability to expand and maintain control over its territories. The Khmer military was well-structured, with a hierarchy that included commanders, soldiers, and specialized units. The army was composed of both professional soldiers and conscripted peasants who were called to serve during times of war.

The Khmer military was known for its versatility and ability to adapt to different combat situations. It included infantry, cavalry, and naval forces, which allowed the empire to conduct campaigns on land and water. Elephants played a significant role in the military, serving as both transport and formidable war machines. These powerful animals were often used to break enemy lines and instill fear in opposing forces.

Expansion through military conquest was a common strategy for the Khmer Empire, enabling it to extend its influence and control over neighboring regions. The empire engaged in numerous military campaigns to subdue rival kingdoms, secure valuable resources, and expand its territorial boundaries. Notable kings, such as Suryavarman II and Jayavarman VII, led successful military campaigns that significantly increased the empire's size and power.

Military victories were often commemorated through grandiose architectural projects and inscriptions that celebrated the king's prowess and divine favor. These monuments served as a reminder of the king's strength and the empire's dominance, reinforcing the social and political hierarchy.

Part 2

Society and Culture

Chapter 1

Social Hierarchy

Class Structure and Social Roles

The Khmer Empire's society was distinctly hierarchical, structured into several classes that determined an individual's role, status, and opportunities. At the top of this social pyramid was the king, considered a divine ruler with absolute authority. Below the king was the royal family, who enjoyed significant privileges and held considerable influence in the empire's political and cultural spheres.

Nobles and high-ranking officials formed the next tier of the hierarchy. These individuals often came from influential families and were appointed to important administrative and military positions. They played a crucial role in governing the empire, managing provinces, and ensuring the king's decrees were implemented. Nobles were also significant landowners, overseeing vast estates and benefiting from the labor and produce of the peasants.

Religious leaders, including priests and monks, held a unique position within Khmer society. They were highly respected and wielded considerable influence due to the intertwined nature of religion and politics. The clergy performed essential religious rituals, provided spiritual guidance, and were often involved in the education of the elite. Temples and monasteries served as centers of learning and cultural preservation.

The artisan and merchant class occupied the middle tier of the social structure. Artisans were skilled craftsmen responsible for the construction of the empire's magnificent temples, sculptures, and intricate carvings. Merchants facilitated trade, both within the empire and with neighboring regions, contributing to the economic prosperity of the Khmer Empire.

At the base of the social pyramid were the commoners, primarily composed of peasants who worked the land. Their labor was the backbone of the empire's agricultural economy, producing the rice and other crops that sustained the population. Despite their low social status, peasants were vital to the empire's stability and growth.

Daily Life of Commoners and Elites

The daily life of commoners in the Khmer Empire was primarily centered around agriculture. Peasants lived in simple wooden or bamboo houses, often located near the fields they cultivated. Their day-to-day activities included planting, tending, and harvesting crops, with rice being the staple food. Peasants also engaged in fishing, hunting, and gathering to supplement their diet. Community life was tightly knit, with extended families living close to one another and supporting each other in daily tasks and rituals.

In contrast, the elite lived more luxurious lives, often residing in grand palaces or well-built homes near urban centers. Their daily routines were less labor-intensive and more focused on administrative duties, cultural activities, and leisure. Nobles and officials would oversee the management of their estates, participate in court life, and engage in religious and ceremonial functions. Education and the arts were highly valued among the elite, with children of noble families receiving instruction in literature, philosophy, and martial skills.

Gender Roles and Family Life

Gender roles in the Khmer Empire were clearly defined but allowed for a certain degree of flexibility. Men typically held positions of power and authority, both in the public and private spheres. They were responsible for governance, military service, and religious duties. In agricultural communities, men performed the physically demanding tasks of plowing and construction.

Women, while generally excluded from formal political and military roles, played a crucial part in both the household and the broader community. In rural areas, women were heavily involved in farming activities, including planting, weeding, and harvesting crops. They also managed household chores, cared for children, and participated in local markets. In urban settings, women could be found working as traders, artisans, and entertainers.

Family life was central to Khmer society, with extended families often living together or in close proximity. Marriages were typically arranged, with families negotiating alliances to strengthen social and economic ties. The birth of children was highly celebrated, and both parents shared responsibilities for raising them, although gender-specific roles influenced their upbringing. Boys were often groomed for roles in agriculture, administration, or religious service, while girls were taught domestic skills and sometimes crafts or trade.

Despite the patriarchal nature of Khmer society, women could achieve significant influence, particularly through their roles in religion and commerce. Some historical records suggest that women of noble birth could wield considerable power within the royal court and even influence political decisions.

Chapter 2

Religion and Spirituality

Hindu Influences and the Role of Vishnu

The Khmer Empire's religious landscape was deeply influenced by Hinduism, particularly during its early and peak periods. Hinduism, introduced through Indian traders and cultural exchange, became the state religion and significantly shaped the empire's spiritual and cultural identity. The Khmer kings embraced Hinduism, considering themselves as divine rulers, often associated with Hindu deities, especially Vishnu and Shiva.

Vishnu, the preserver god in the Hindu trinity, held a prominent place in Khmer spirituality. Many temples, including the magnificent Angkor Wat, were dedicated to Vishnu. These structures symbolized the cosmic order and the king's divine right to rule. Vishnu's role as a protector resonated with the Khmer rulers' need to legitimize their power and maintain stability in their realm.

The worship of Vishnu involved elaborate rituals and ceremonies conducted by priests in grand temples adorned with intricate carvings and statues depicting the god. Devotees offered prayers, flowers, and food to the deity, seeking blessings for prosperity, protection, and good fortune. The temples themselves were considered earthly abodes of the gods, serving as centers of both religious and political power.

Transition to Buddhism

In the late 12th century, a significant religious shift occurred under the reign of King Jayavarman VII, who embraced Mahayana Buddhism. This transition marked a profound transformation in the spiritual and cultural landscape of the Khmer Empire. Jayavarman VII, revered as a compassionate and enlightened ruler, promoted Buddhism as the state religion, which emphasized the principles of compassion, altruism, and the pursuit of enlightenment.

The transition from Hinduism to Buddhism did not happen abruptly but rather evolved gradually. Many Hindu temples were converted to Buddhist shrines, and new Buddhist temples and monasteries were constructed. Iconography and temple architecture began to reflect Buddhist themes, with images of the Buddha and bodhisattvas becoming prominent.

Buddhism's inclusive and accessible nature resonated with the common people, fostering a sense of spiritual community and social harmony. Monasteries played a crucial role in education, healthcare, and social welfare, contributing to the overall well-being of the populace. The Buddhist emphasis on moral conduct, meditation, and the pursuit of wisdom influenced daily life and governance, promoting a more compassionate and ethical society.

Religious Practices and Rituals

Religious practices and rituals in the Khmer Empire were diverse and reflected the syncretic nature of Khmer spirituality, blending Hindu and Buddhist traditions. During the Hindu period, temple rituals were elaborate and involved complex ceremonies led by priests. These rituals included offerings, recitations of sacred texts, and the performance of symbolic acts to invoke the blessings of the gods.

Festivals and religious observances were integral to Khmer religious life. Celebrations such as the annual temple festival (Bon Om Touk) and the royal coronation ceremonies were marked by grand processions, music, dance, and communal feasting. These events reinforced social cohesion and the divine status of the king.

With the advent of Buddhism, religious practices became more focused on individual spiritual development and community service. Monastic life flourished, with monks dedicating themselves to meditation, study, and teaching. Laypeople supported the monastic community through alms-giving and participating in communal rituals.

Key Buddhist rituals included the chanting of sutras, meditation sessions, and merit-making activities such as building stupas and offering donations to temples. The construction of stupas and statues of the Buddha became acts of devotion, symbolizing the impermanence of life and the aspiration for enlightenment.

Pilgrimage also played a significant role in religious practice. Sacred sites such as Angkor Wat and the Bayon temple complex attracted pilgrims from within the empire and beyond, fostering a sense of spiritual connection and cultural unity.

Chapter 3

Language and Literature

The Khmer Script and Language

The Khmer script, an abugida developed from the Pallava script of South India, is one of the oldest scripts in Southeast Asia and played a crucial role in the cultural and administrative functions of the Khmer Empire. This script was adapted to write the Khmer language, which is part of the Austroasiatic language family and remains the official language of Cambodia today.

The Khmer script is characterized by its intricate and ornate characters, which were meticulously inscribed on temple walls, steles, and other monuments. The script consists of consonants, vowels, and various diacritical marks, making it highly versatile for expressing the phonetic nuances of the Khmer language.

Language in the Khmer Empire was more than just a means of communication; it was a powerful tool for governance, religion, and cultural expression. Sanskrit, the classical language of Hinduism and Buddhism, was also extensively used, particularly in religious and royal inscriptions. Sanskrit's use signified the empire's connection to the broader Indian cultural and spiritual traditions.

Important Literary Works and Inscriptions

Inscriptions on stone, known as steles, are among the most significant literary artifacts from the Khmer Empire. These inscriptions provide invaluable insights into the political, religious, and social life of the empire. They typically recorded royal decrees, religious dedications, land grants, and historical events.

One of the most famous inscriptions is the "Preah Ko Preah Keo" inscription at the Bakong temple, which dates back to the reign of King Indravarman I. This inscription not only commemorates the king's religious endowments but also provides a detailed account of the construction of the temple and the socio-political context of the time.

The epigraphic records from the reign of Jayavarman VII are particularly noteworthy. His reign saw the proliferation of Buddhist inscriptions, reflecting the transition from Hinduism to Mahayana Buddhism. The Ta Prohm inscription, for instance, lists the temple's extensive holdings and the vast number of people associated with its upkeep, highlighting the temple's significance as both a religious and economic center.

Literary works, while not as abundant as inscriptions, also played a role in the cultural heritage of the Khmer Empire. These included religious texts, royal edicts, and poetic compositions, often written in both Khmer and Sanskrit. These texts were instrumental in preserving and transmitting religious teachings, moral values, and historical narratives.

Education and Dissemination of Knowledge

Education in the Khmer Empire was closely linked to religious institutions, primarily temples and monasteries. These centers of learning were responsible for educating monks and, to some extent, the laity in religious doctrines, moral philosophy, and practical skills.

Monasteries served as the primary educational institutions where young boys, especially those from elite families, received instruction in the Khmer script, religious texts, and classical languages like Sanskrit and Pali. Education in these institutions was not only about religious training but also encompassed broader subjects such as astronomy, medicine, and law.

The dissemination of knowledge was facilitated through oral traditions and the meticulous copying of manuscripts. Monks played a vital role in this process, acting as both teachers and scribes. The knowledge preserved in these manuscripts was essential for the administration of the empire, the practice of religion, and the maintenance of cultural identity.

Public education, though limited, was available in some form through communal gatherings and temple schools. These schools provided basic literacy and religious education to the general populace, ensuring that essential cultural and moral values were passed down through generations.

The role of literature and inscriptions in the Khmer Empire extended beyond mere record-keeping. They were integral to the empire's identity, serving as a testament to its grandeur, spiritual devotion, and intellectual achievements. Through the preservation of language and literature, the Khmer Empire left an enduring legacy that continues to influence Cambodian culture and society today.

Part 3

Architectural Marvels

Chapter 1

Angkor Wat

History and Construction

Angkor Wat, the crown jewel of the Khmer Empire's architectural achievements, stands as the largest religious monument in the world. Constructed in the early 12th century during the reign of King Suryavarman II, Angkor Wat was originally dedicated to the Hindu god Vishnu. The temple's construction spanned approximately 30 years, reflecting the Khmer Empire's immense resources, advanced engineering skills, and deep religious devotion.

The construction of Angkor Wat involved a massive workforce, including skilled architects, artisans, and laborers. Sandstone blocks, the primary building material, were quarried from the Kulen Hills and transported via an extensive network of canals. The precise cutting and fitting of these blocks, without the use of mortar, demonstrate the remarkable craftsmanship of the Khmer builders.

Architectural Design and Symbolism

Angkor Wat's architectural design is a masterpiece of symmetry, proportion, and symbolism. The temple is designed to represent Mount Meru, the mythical center of the universe in Hindu and Buddhist cosmology. The central tower, rising

65 meters above the ground, symbolizes Mount Meru's peak, while the surrounding towers represent the mountain's smaller peaks.

The layout of Angkor Wat follows a concentric pattern with three rectangular galleries, each one progressively higher than the one below. This design not only creates a sense of ascending grandeur but also symbolizes the journey from the earthly realm to the divine. The temple's orientation towards the west, unusual for Hindu temples, has been interpreted as a reference to Vishnu's association with the west and as a symbolic representation of death and the afterlife.

The bas-reliefs that adorn Angkor Wat's walls are some of the finest examples of Khmer art. These intricate carvings depict scenes from Hindu epics such as the Ramayana and the Mahabharata, as well as historical events and celestial beings. The "Churning of the Ocean of Milk," a central myth in Hindu cosmology, is one of the most famous bas-reliefs, illustrating the eternal struggle between good and evil and the quest for immortality.

Religious Significance and Cultural Impact

Angkor Wat's religious significance extends beyond its initial dedication to Vishnu. In the late 13th century, the temple transitioned from Hinduism to Theravada Buddhism, reflecting the broader religious shift within the Khmer Empire. This transformation involves the addition of Buddhist statues and the repurposing of Hindu iconography to fit

Buddhist narratives, showcasing the temple's adaptability and enduring spiritual importance.

As a center of religious activity, Angkor Wat played a crucial role in the spiritual life of the Khmer people. It served as a pilgrimage site, a place of worship, and a venue for religious ceremonies. The temple's design, with its numerous galleries and courtyards, facilitated the congregation of large numbers of devotees, highlighting its importance as a communal and sacred space.

Culturally, Angkor Wat has had a profound impact on Cambodian identity and heritage. It is a symbol of national pride, representing the ingenuity and grandeur of the Khmer civilization. The temple has inspired countless works of art, literature, and folklore, embedding itself in the cultural consciousness of Cambodia and beyond.

In modern times, Angkor Wat continues to captivate visitors from around the world. Its inclusion on the UNESCO World Heritage list in 1992 has helped to preserve and promote the temple, ensuring its legacy endures. Efforts by the Cambodian government and international organizations to restore and maintain Angkor Wat underscore its significance as both a historical monument and a living cultural treasure.

Angkor Wat's blend of architectural brilliance, symbolic depth, and religious significance makes it a unique and enduring testament to the Khmer Empire's artistic and spiritual achievements. Its towering spires and intricate carvings continue to inspire awe and reverence, inviting visitors to explore the rich history and cultural heritage of one of the world's greatest civilizations.

Chapter 2

Angkor Thom and the Bayon Temple

Founding and Historical Significance

Angkor Thom, meaning "Great City," served as the last and most enduring capital of the Khmer Empire. Founded in the late 12th century by King Jayavarman VII, Angkor Thom was constructed on an even grander scale than its predecessor, encompassing an area of approximately 9 square kilometers and housing a population estimated at over one million people.

The construction of Angkor Thom was a monumental undertaking, involving extensive urban planning, infrastructure development, and architectural innovation. The city was surrounded by a massive moat and fortified by high walls, with five monumental gates providing access to the inner sanctum. Each gate was adorned with intricately carved towers and causeways lined with stone figures of gods and demons, symbolizing the cosmic struggle between good and evil.

Architectural Highlights and the Enigmatic Smiling Faces

At the heart of Angkor Thom lies the Bayon Temple, renowned for its iconic smiling faces and intricate bas-reliefs. Built in the late 12th century by King Jayavarman VII, the Bayon is characterized by its central tower, which is surrounded by 54 smaller towers adorned with enigmatic faces thought to represent the bodhisattva Avalokiteshvara or the king himself.

The faces of the Bayon are one of the most enigmatic and captivating features of the temple complex. Carved with serene expressions and downcast eyes, these faces are believed to embody qualities of compassion, wisdom, and equanimity. Their enigmatic smiles have puzzled scholars and visitors alike, inviting speculation about their meaning and significance.

In addition to its iconic faces, the Bayon is adorned with intricate bas-reliefs depicting scenes from Khmer daily life, historical events, and religious mythology. These carvings provide valuable insights into the cultural, social, and religious context of the Khmer Empire, showcasing the artistic skill and craftsmanship of the Khmer artisans.

Cultural and Religious Importance

Angkor Thom and the Bayon Temple played a central role in the religious and cultural life of the Khmer Empire. As the political and spiritual heart of the empire, Angkor Thom served as a symbol of royal power and divine authority. The Bayon, with its imposing presence and spiritual significance, was a place of worship, meditation, and pilgrimage for Khmer kings, nobles, and commoners alike.

The architectural and artistic achievements of Angkor Thom and the Bayon Temple reflect the synthesis of Hinduism and Buddhism that characterized the Khmer Empire. While the Bayon is primarily associated with Buddhist iconography and symbolism, elements of Hindu mythology and cosmology are also present, highlighting the eclectic and inclusive nature of Khmer religious practice.

In modern times, Angkor Thom and the Bayon Temple continue to inspire wonder and admiration among visitors from around the world. Their timeless beauty, profound symbolism, and rich historical legacy serve as a reminder of the enduring cultural heritage of the Khmer people and their remarkable civilization.

Chapter 3

Other Significant Temples

Ta Prohm and Its Unique Features

Ta Prohm, built in the late 12th and early 13th centuries by King Jayavarman VII, is renowned for its unique fusion of nature and architecture. Unlike many other temples in the Angkor complex, Ta Prohm has been left in a state of semi-ruin, with towering trees and giant roots intertwining with the ancient stone structures. This harmonious coexistence of man-made and natural elements gives Ta Prohm its distinctive and evocative atmosphere, earning it the nickname "The Jungle Temple."

One of the most iconic features of Ta Prohm is the sight of massive silk-cotton and strangler fig trees growing directly out of the temple walls, their roots enveloping doorways, courtyards, and corridors in a tangled embrace. This dramatic interplay between nature and architecture has captivated visitors for centuries, inspiring awe and wonder at the power and resilience of the natural world.

Banteay Srei's Detailed Carvings

Banteay Srei, located approximately 25 kilometers northeast of the main Angkor complex, is renowned for its exquisite and intricate carvings. Built in the 10th century by King

Rajendravarman II, Banteay Srei is dedicated to the Hindu god Shiva and is celebrated for the quality and craftsmanship of its sandstone carvings, which are among the finest examples of classical Khmer art.

The carvings at Banteay Srei depict scenes from Hindu mythology, including epic battles, divine rituals, and celestial beings. Each intricately carved relief is characterized by its delicate detail, refined composition, and expressive storytelling, showcasing the skill and artistry of the Khmer artisans who created them. The temple's walls, lintels, and pediments are adorned with an astonishing array of decorative motifs, including floral patterns, mythical creatures, and celestial dancers, all rendered with remarkable precision and finesse.

Preah Khan and Its Historical Background

Preah Khan, meaning "Sacred Sword," was built in the late 12th century by King Jayavarman VII as a Buddhist monastery and educational institution. Located northeast of Angkor Thom, Preah Khan served as a center of learning, meditation, and religious practice, housing hundreds of monks and scholars within its vast complex of courtyards, galleries, and pavilions.

The temple's name, Preah Khan, is believed to be a reference to the mythical sword of King Jayavarman VII, which he used to liberate Cambodia from foreign invaders and restore peace and prosperity to the kingdom. As a symbol of royal power and divine protection, Preah Khan was endowed with lavish patronage and endowed with richly decorated sculptures, inscriptions, and architectural elements, reflecting the grandeur and magnificence of the Khmer Empire at its zenith.

Today, Ta Prohm, Banteay Srei, and Preah Khan continue to fascinate and inspire visitors with their unique beauty, historical significance, and cultural resonance. As enduring symbols of the Khmer Empire's artistic and architectural achievements, these temples stand as testaments to the ingenuity, creativity, and spiritual devotion of the Khmer people, preserving their legacy for future generations to admire and appreciate.

Part 4

Art and Iconography

Chapter 1

Sculpture and Bas-Reliefs

Artistic Styles and Influences

Khmer sculpture and bas-reliefs represent a rich tapestry of artistic styles and influences that evolved over the centuries, blending indigenous Khmer traditions with elements borrowed from Indian, Chinese, and Southeast Asian cultures. From the intricate carvings of the pre-Angkor period to the monumental sculptures of the Angkor era, Khmer art reflects a synthesis of diverse cultural influences and artistic techniques, characterized by its exquisite craftsmanship, refined aesthetics, and spiritual symbolism.

The earliest Khmer sculptures date back to the 7th century, influenced by Indian artistic traditions introduced through trade and cultural exchange. These early sculptures, predominantly made of sandstone, exhibit stylistic elements reminiscent of Indian Gupta and Pallava art, characterized by graceful proportions, serene expressions, and symbolic gestures known as mudras. Over time, Khmer artists developed their own distinctive style, incorporating local motifs and iconography to create a unique Khmer aesthetic that would reach its zenith during the Angkor period.

Depictions of Deities and Mythological Events

Khmer sculpture and bas-reliefs are replete with depictions of Hindu gods, goddesses, and mythological events, reflecting the profound influence of Hinduism on Khmer religion, art, and culture. At temples such as Angkor Wat and Angkor Thom, colossal statues of Hindu deities such as Vishnu, Shiva, and Brahma tower over devotees, their divine attributes and attributes symbolizing cosmic order, creation, and destruction.

Bas-reliefs, intricately carved onto temple walls and galleries, depict epic scenes from Hindu mythology, including the churning of the ocean of milk, the battle between gods and demons, and the divine deeds of Vishnu and Shiva. These narrative reliefs, executed with remarkable detail and dynamism, serve as visual narratives that illustrate the fundamental tenets of Hindu cosmology, morality, and spirituality, conveying complex theological concepts in accessible and engaging ways.

Symbolism in Khmer Art

Khmer art is imbued with rich symbolism and allegory, conveying deeper layers of meaning and significance beyond mere representation. Every element of Khmer sculpture and bas-reliefs, from the posture of deities to the iconographic attributes of mythical creatures, carries symbolic weight and spiritual resonance, reflecting the Khmer worldview and religious beliefs.

The lotus flower, for example, symbolizes purity and enlightenment, often depicted in the hands of divine beings such as Avalokiteshvara and Tara. The naga, a mythical serpent often depicted as a protective deity, symbolizes fertility, abundance, and divine kingship, its multi-headed form representing the cosmic forces of creation and destruction. Other symbols, such as the wheel of dharma, the sacred bull Nandi, and the cosmic dancer Nataraja, convey profound philosophical concepts and spiritual truths, inviting viewers to contemplate the mysteries of existence and the nature of reality.

Chapter 2

Dance and Performance

Traditional Khmer Dance Forms

Khmer dance, one of the oldest performing arts in Southeast Asia, embodies the grace, elegance, and spiritual depth of Khmer culture. Rooted in ancient rituals and courtly traditions, Khmer dance encompasses a diverse range of classical and folk forms, each characterized by its distinctive movements, gestures, and music.

- Apsara Dance: The apsara dance, inspired by celestial nymphs from Hindu mythology, is perhaps the most iconic and revered form of Khmer classical dance. Dancers, adorned in elaborate costumes and headdresses, evoke the ethereal beauty and divine grace of apsara beings through intricate hand gestures, fluid movements, and mesmerizing choreography. Apsara dance performances, often staged at temple complexes such as Angkor Wat, serve as a tribute to Cambodia's cultural heritage and artistic legacy.
- Robam Tep Apsara: Robam tep apsara, or the dance of the celestial nymphs, is a refined and sophisticated form of Khmer court dance that originated in the royal courts of Angkor. Dancers, dressed in traditional silk sarongs and ornate jewelry, perform intricate sequences of gestures and poses that evoke the divine

attributes and celestial splendor of apsara beings. Robam tep apsara is characterized by its graceful movements, subtle expressions, and intricate footwork, reflecting the aristocratic refinement and spiritual symbolism of Khmer court culture.

- Robam Preah Reach Trop: Robam preah reach trop, or the dance of the royal khmer, is a ceremonial dance performed during royal festivals and state occasions. Dancers, dressed in regal attire adorned with gold and jewels, enact scenes from Khmer mythology and history, paying homage to the kingdom's legendary monarchs and heroic figures. Robam preah reach trop combines elements of classical dance, martial arts, and dramatic storytelling, showcasing the splendor and majesty of Khmer royal tradition.

Cultural Significance of Performances

Khmer dance performances play a central role in Cambodia's cultural and religious life, serving as a vibrant expression of national identity, spiritual devotion, and community cohesion. From temple ceremonies and royal processions to village festivals and social gatherings, dance performances are woven into the fabric of Khmer society, connecting people to their heritage and shared traditions.

- Religious Rituals: Khmer dance has deep roots in religious rituals and ceremonial practices, serving as a form of devotional expression and spiritual invocation. Apsara dance, for example, is often performed as part of religious ceremonies and temple festivals, where dancers embody divine beings and celestial guardians to invoke blessings and protection.

- Celebratory Festivals: Khmer dance is also a key feature of celebratory festivals and seasonal events, where communities come together to honor their ancestors, commemorate historical events, and celebrate the cycles of nature. Traditional dances such as robam tep apsara and robam preah reach trop are performed during Khmer New Year, Water Festival, and other auspicious occasions, bringing joy, color, and vitality to communal festivities.

Costumes and Musical Instruments

Khmer dance is distinguished by its elaborate costumes, intricate jewelry, and ornate headdresses, which are designed to evoke the opulence and grandeur of Khmer court culture. Dancers wear traditional silk sarongs, embellished with intricate patterns and motifs inspired by Khmer art and architecture, along with elaborate headpieces adorned with flowers, feathers, and gemstones. Jewelry, including gold bracelets, anklets, and necklaces, completes the ensemble, adding a touch of regal elegance and artistic sophistication.

In addition to costumes, Khmer dance is accompanied by traditional musical instruments, including the pinpeat ensemble, a unique ensemble of percussion and wind instruments that provides the rhythmic and melodic accompaniment for dance performances. The pinpeat ensemble typically includes instruments such as the roneat (xylophone), chhing (cymbals), sralai (oboe), and kong vong thom (large gong), which together create a rich tapestry of sound that enhances the beauty and expressiveness of Khmer dance.

Part 5

Economy and Trade

Chapter 1

Agricultural Practices

Rice Cultivation and Irrigation Systems

Rice cultivation formed the backbone of the Khmer Empire's economy, providing sustenance for its burgeoning population and serving as a vital source of wealth and prosperity. The fertile floodplains of the Mekong and Tonle Sap rivers offered ideal conditions for rice cultivation, enabling Khmer farmers to harness the region's abundant water resources and fertile soil to cultivate rice on a massive scale.

- Terraced Fields: Khmer farmers developed sophisticated irrigation systems to regulate water flow and maximize agricultural productivity. One of the most remarkable engineering achievements of the Khmer Empire was the construction of vast networks of reservoirs, canals, and reservoirs, which enabled farmers to control flooding, manage water levels, and irrigate rice fields year-round. Terraced fields, carved into the landscape in concentric circles or stepped tiers, allowed farmers to cultivate rice on hilly terrain and minimize soil erosion, ensuring a steady supply of rice for both subsistence and surplus.
- Baray Reservoirs: Baray reservoirs, immense artificial lakes constructed by Khmer engineers, played a crucial role in rice cultivation and water management.

These vast reservoirs, some spanning several square kilometers in area, served as catchment basins for monsoon rains, storing water during the wet season and releasing it gradually during the dry season to irrigate rice fields downstream. Baray reservoirs were not only vital for agricultural irrigation but also served as centers of religious worship, pilgrimage, and social gathering, symbolizing the Khmer Empire's mastery of hydraulic engineering and its close relationship with the natural environment.

Other Crops and Livestock

While rice was the primary staple crop of the Khmer Empire, farmers also cultivated a diverse range of other crops to supplement their diet and diversify their agricultural output. Alongside rice, Khmer farmers grew crops such as maize, millet, beans, and root vegetables, which provided essential nutrients, dietary variety, and resilience against crop failure. Fruit orchards, including mango, banana, and citrus trees, were cultivated in orchards and gardens, providing additional sources of food and income for rural communities.

In addition to crop cultivation, Khmer farmers practiced animal husbandry, raising livestock such as cattle, water buffalo, pigs, and poultry to meet their protein needs, provide draft power for agriculture, and generate additional income through trade and commerce. Water buffalo, in particular, played a vital role in rice cultivation, plowing fields, and hauling agricultural produce to market, while pigs and poultry were reared for meat, eggs, and other animal products.

Innovations in Agriculture

The Khmer Empire was renowned for its innovative agricultural practices and engineering feats, which enabled it to sustain a large population and support a thriving economy. In addition to terraced fields and baray reservoirs, Khmer farmers developed advanced techniques for soil conservation, crop rotation, and land management, which helped to maintain soil fertility, prevent erosion, and maximize agricultural yields. The use of organic fertilizers, such as compost and animal manure, enriched the soil and enhanced crop productivity, while the construction of check dams and irrigation channels facilitated water distribution and flood control, ensuring the resilience and sustainability of Khmer agriculture.

Furthermore, the Khmer Empire's extensive network of roads, bridges, and waterways facilitated the transport and distribution of agricultural produce, enabling surplus crops to be transported from rural hinterlands to urban centers and distant markets. Trade routes such as the Silk Road and maritime routes connecting Southeast Asia with India, China, and the Middle East facilitated the exchange of goods, ideas, and technologies, enriching Khmer society and stimulating economic growth and cultural exchange.

Chapter 2

Trade and Commerce

Internal and External Trade Routes

The Khmer Empire was a flourishing center of trade and commerce, both within its vast territorial domains and with neighboring regions across Southeast Asia and beyond. A network of well-established trade routes, both land and maritime, facilitated the exchange of goods, ideas, and cultures, fostering economic prosperity and cultural exchange throughout the empire.

- **Land Trade Routes:** The Khmer Empire's extensive network of roads and pathways connected its urban centers, rural hinterlands, and distant provinces, facilitating the movement of goods and people across the empire. Major land trade routes extended from Angkor, the imperial capital, to provincial capitals such as Battambang, Siem Reap, and Kampong Thom, as well as to neighboring kingdoms and empires such as Champa, Dai Viet, and the Malay Peninsula. These overland trade routes were vital arteries of commerce, linking agricultural heartlands with urban markets, religious pilgrimage sites, and strategic military outposts, and enabling the flow of commodities such as rice, textiles, pottery, metals, and luxury goods between different regions and social groups.

- **Maritime Trade Routes:** In addition to land routes, the Khmer Empire developed extensive maritime trade networks, leveraging its strategic location along the Gulf of Thailand and the South China Sea to engage in maritime commerce with neighboring politics in Southeast Asia and beyond. Coastal cities such as Oc Eo, Sambor Prei Kuk, and Kampong Cham served as important entrepôts and trading hubs, connecting the mainland with maritime trade routes linking the Indian Ocean with the South China Sea. Khmer merchant ships, known as junks, plied these maritime highways, carrying cargoes of spices, precious metals, gemstones, ceramics, silks, and other exotic goods to distant ports of call in India, China, Java, Sumatra, and beyond. Maritime trade brought wealth and prosperity to the Khmer Empire, enriching its cities, stimulating economic growth, and fostering cultural exchange and diplomatic relations with foreign powers.

Goods Traded and Economic Impact

The Khmer Empire's vibrant trade networks facilitated the exchange of a wide range of commodities, reflecting the empire's economic diversity, cultural sophistication, and geopolitical importance within the broader Indian Ocean world. Some of the most sought-after goods traded by the Khmer Empire included:

- **Agricultural Products:** Rice, the staple crop of the Khmer Empire, was a major commodity traded both domestically and internationally, providing sustenance for urban populations and generating surplus for export. Other agricultural products traded by the Khmer Empire included spices (such as pepper, cardamom, and cinnamon), fruits (such as mangoes, bananas, and durians), vegetables (such as cucumbers, squash, and beans), and medicinal herbs (such as ginger, turmeric, and lemongrass).

- **Luxury Goods:** The Khmer Empire was renowned for its production of luxury goods, including textiles, ceramics, metalwork, and jewelry, which were highly prized commodities traded with foreign merchants and aristocrats. Khmer silk textiles, renowned for their exquisite craftsmanship and intricate designs, were in high demand throughout Southeast Asia and beyond, serving as symbols of wealth, status, and cultural prestige. Khmer ceramics, characterized by their distinctive shapes, glazes, and motifs, were exported to distant markets in China, India, and the Middle East, where they were prized for their beauty and craftsmanship.

- **Precious Metals and Gemstones:** The Khmer Empire was rich in natural resources, including precious metals such as gold, silver, and copper, which were mined from the empire's mountainous hinterlands and traded as bullion or crafted into jewelry, religious artifacts, and decorative objects. Gemstones such as rubies, sapphires, and emeralds were also highly valued commodities traded by the

Khmer Empire, sourced from mines in present-day Cambodia, Myanmar, and Thailand, and exported to international markets for use in jewelry, sculpture, and religious iconography.

Role of Merchants and Trade Centers

Merchants played a crucial role in the Khmer Empire's economy, serving as intermediaries and facilitators of trade between producers and consumers, urban centers and rural hinterlands, and local markets and international ports. Khmer merchants, organized into guilds and trading associations, operated a variety of trade routes and commercial enterprises, engaging in both wholesale and retail trade, barter and currency exchange, and import and export transactions.

Trade centers such as Angkor, the imperial capital of the Khmer Empire, served as focal points of commercial activity, attracting merchants, artisans, and pilgrims from across the empire and beyond. The bustling markets of Angkor, including the Central Market (Psah Thmei), the Old Market (Psah Chas), and the Night Market (Psah Nat), offered a dazzling array of goods and services, ranging from foodstuffs and household goods to luxury items and exotic imports. In addition to Angkor, other important trade centers in the Khmer Empire included provincial capitals such as Yasodharapura (present-day Siem Reap), Hariharalaya (present-day Roluos), and Mahendraparvata (present-day Phnom Kulen), as well as coastal ports such as Oc Eo, Sambor Prei Kuk, and Kampong Cham.

Part 6

The Fall of the Khmer Empire

Chapter 1

Causes of Decline

The decline and eventual collapse of the Khmer Empire marked the end of a glorious era in Southeast Asian history, characterized by political power, cultural splendor, and architectural grandeur. However, numerous internal and external factors contributed to the empire's decline, leading to its eventual fragmentation and disintegration.

Internal Strife and Political Instability

One of the primary causes of the Khmer Empire's decline was internal strife and political instability within the empire itself. As the empire expanded and centralized power in the hands of the monarch, tensions often arose between rival factions within the royal court, leading to court intrigues, power struggles, and succession crises. Factionalism and infighting among the ruling elite weakened the central government's authority and undermined its ability to govern effectively, eroding public confidence in the state and sowing seeds of discontent among the populace. Moreover, the absence of clear rules of succession and mechanisms for peaceful transfer of power often resulted in dynastic disputes and civil wars, further destabilizing the empire and hastening its decline.

External Invasions and Conflicts

In addition to internal strife, the Khmer Empire faced numerous external threats from neighboring kingdoms and empires, which sought to challenge its hegemony and expand their own territories at its expense. Throughout its history, the Khmer Empire engaged in frequent conflicts and wars with rival powers such as the Cham, the Vietnamese, the Siamese, and the Burmese, who coveted its wealth, resources, and strategic position in the region. These external invasions and conflicts drained the empire's military and economic resources, weakened its defenses, and exposed its vulnerabilities to further aggression and conquest. Moreover, the constant warfare and instability along the empire's frontiers disrupted trade, agriculture, and commerce, leading to economic decline and social upheaval.

Environmental Factors and Resource Depletion

Another significant factor contributing to the Khmer Empire's decline was environmental degradation and resource depletion, resulting from unsustainable land use practices, deforestation, and hydraulic engineering projects. The empire's rapid population growth, urbanization, and agricultural expansion placed immense pressure on its natural ecosystems, leading to widespread deforestation, soil erosion, and loss of biodiversity. Large-scale irrigation projects such as the construction of reservoirs, canals, and water management systems, while initially beneficial for agricultural productivity and food security, ultimately led to soil salinization, waterlogging, and ecological imbalances, undermining the empire's long-term sustainability and resilience.

Chapter 2

The Aftermath

The collapse of the Khmer Empire in the 15th century marked the end of an era of grandeur and cultural flourishing in Southeast Asia. However, despite its demise, the legacy of the empire continues to resonate in modern Cambodia and beyond, shaping the country's cultural identity, architectural heritage, and historical consciousness.

The Legacy of the Khmer Empire in Modern Cambodia

The legacy of the Khmer Empire remains deeply ingrained in the cultural fabric of modern Cambodia, serving as a source of national pride and identity for its people. The iconic Angkor temples, with their intricate carvings, majestic spires, and spiritual significance, stand as enduring symbols of the empire's glory and achievements, attracting millions of visitors from around the world each year. Moreover, the Khmer language, customs, and traditions continue to thrive in contemporary Cambodian society, reflecting the enduring influence of the empire on the country's cultural heritage.

Rediscovery and Restoration Efforts

In the 19th century, the rediscovery of the Angkor temples by European explorers such as Henri Mouhot sparked renewed interest in the Khmer Empire and its architectural wonders. Subsequent archaeological excavations and restoration efforts, led by organizations such as the École française d'Extrême-Orient (EFEO) and the UNESCO World Heritage Centre, have helped to preserve and protect these ancient monuments for future generations. Through meticulous conservation work and site management initiatives, experts have sought to safeguard the Angkor temples from the ravages of time, environmental degradation, and tourism-related pressures, ensuring their survival as a testament to human ingenuity and creativity.

Ongoing Challenges and Preservation Efforts

Despite ongoing preservation efforts, the Angkor temples continue to face numerous challenges, including vandalism, looting, illegal encroachment, and environmental degradation. Rapid urbanization, population growth, and infrastructure development in the surrounding area have also posed threats to the integrity of the archaeological sites and their surrounding ecosystems. Moreover, the impacts of climate change, such as rising temperatures, extreme weather events, and water scarcity, further exacerbate the vulnerability of the Angkor complex to environmental risks and natural disasters.

In response to these challenges, various stakeholders, including the Cambodian government, international organizations, NGOs, and local communities, have collaborated to implement comprehensive conservation and management strategies aimed at safeguarding the Angkor temples and their surrounding cultural landscape. These efforts include the establishment of protected areas, the enforcement of heritage laws, community engagement and capacity-building initiatives, and sustainable tourism practices designed to balance the preservation of cultural heritage with the socio-economic needs of local communities.

Conclusion

In the course of this exploration into the rich history and cultural legacy of the Khmer Empire, we have journeyed through the majestic temples of Angkor, delved into the intricacies of Khmer society and culture, and reflected on the empire's enduring impact on the modern world. As we conclude our journey, let us recapitulate the key points discussed and reflect on the importance of preserving this invaluable heritage for future generations.

Summary of Key Points

Throughout history, the Khmer Empire emerged as a beacon of civilization in Southeast Asia, renowned for its architectural marvels, religious fervor, and artistic achievements. From the grandeur of Angkor Wat to the enigmatic smiles of the Bayon Temple, the empire's legacy continues to captivate the imagination of scholars, travelers, and admirers around the globe. Through its political prowess, cultural patronage, and economic prosperity, the Khmer Empire left an indelible mark on the region, shaping the course of history for centuries to come.

The Importance of Preservation

Preserving the cultural heritage of the Khmer Empire is paramount to safeguarding the identity and legacy of the Cambodian people and honoring the contributions of one of history's greatest civilizations. Despite the passage of time and the challenges of modernity, ongoing efforts to conserve and protect the Angkor temples and other Khmer sites remain critical to ensuring their survival for future generations. By recognizing the significance of these ancient treasures and advocating for their preservation, we can help to safeguard this priceless heritage for posterity.

How Readers Can Contribute to Preservation

As stewards of cultural heritage, readers can play a vital role in supporting preservation efforts for Khmer heritage. Whether through raising awareness, participating in volunteer programs, or making responsible choices as travelers, individuals can contribute to the conservation and sustainable management of archaeological sites, historic monuments, and cultural landscapes. By respecting local communities, following ethical tourism practices, and advocating for heritage protection, readers can help to ensure that the legacy of the Khmer Empire endures for generations to come.

Final Thoughts

As we conclude our exploration of the Khmer Empire, let us reflect on the enduring legacy of this remarkable civilization and the profound impact it has had on the cultural, artistic, and spiritual traditions of Southeast Asia. From the towering temples of Angkor to the vibrant cultural heritage of modern Cambodia, the spirit of the Khmer Empire lives on in the hearts and minds of people around the world. As we bid farewell to this ancient kingdom, let us carry forward its legacy of innovation, creativity, and resilience, and continue to explore, celebrate, and preserve the wonders of Khmer heritage for all to enjoy.

In the words of the great Khmer king Jayavarman VII, "May the blessings of the gods be upon you, and may your journey be filled with discovery, enlightenment, and wonder."

End of the Journey

Made in United States
Troutdale, OR
09/27/2024

23188863R00044